GREAT RELIGIOUS LEADERS

Krishna
and
Hinduism

Kerena Marchant

HODDER
Wayland

an imprint of Hodder Children's Books

Great Religious Leaders

Buddha and Buddhism
Guru Nanak and Sikhism
Krishna and Hinduism

Jesus and Christianity
Muhammad and Islam
Moses and Judaism

© White-Thomson Publishing Ltd 2002

Produced for Hodder Wayland by White-Thomson Publishing Ltd.
2/3 St Andrew's Place, Lewes, E Sussex, BN7 1UP, UK

Editor: Margot Richardson
Designer: Jane Hawkins

Graphics and maps: Tim Mayer
Proofreader: Philippa Smith

First published in 2002 by Hodder Wayland, an imprint of Hodder Children's Books

The right of Kerena Marchant to be identified as the author of this Work has been asserted by her in accordance with the Copyright, Designs and Patents Act 1988.

British Library Cataloguing in Publication Data
Marchant, Kerena
    Krishna and Hinduism. – (Great Religious Leaders)
    1. Krishna (Hindu deity) 2. Hinduism I. Title
    294.5
ISBN 0 7502 3700 7

Hodder Children's Books
A division of Hodder Headline Ltd
338 Euston Road, London NW1 3BH

Cover top: Krishna blessing Arjun at the battle of Kurukshetra
Cover main: Worshippers at a Krishna temple, Vrindavan, India
Title page: Hindu women bathing in the sacred River Ganges.

Picture Acknowledgements: The publisher would like to thank the following for permission to reproduce their pictures: AKG 7 (Jean-Louis Nou), 8 (Jean-Louis Nou), 11, 28 (Jean-Louis Nou), 43 (top) (Jean-Louis Nou); Art Directors and Trip Photo Library *cover top* (T Luther), 9 (H Rogers), 14 (Dinodia), 16 (T Luther), 17 (Dindodia), 18 (H Luther), 20 (Dinodia), 21 (top) (T Luther), 30 (H Rogers), 32(Dinodia), 34 (C Wormald), 33 (Resource Foto), 36 (Dinodia), 39 (Dinodia), 40 (C Wormald), 41 (Dinodia); Chapel Studios 15 (Bob Brecher); Eye Ubiquitous *title page* (David Cumming), 22 (David Cumming), 23 (Bennett Dean), 27 (Chris Fairclough); Hodder Wayland Picture Library 21 (bottom); Images of India 42 (Melind A Ketkar); Impact 19 (Daniel White), 38 (Daniel White); Christine Osborne 4, 25, 31, Panos Pictures 44 (Piers Benatari); Anne and Bury Peerless 10, 12, 13; Pictorial Press 45 (???); White-Thomson Publishing *cover main*, 19, 24, 26, 29, 33, 37, 43 (bottom) (all Chris Fairclough).

Contents

What is Hinduism?

Hinduism is the oldest religion in the world. It began about 3000BCE in an area around the river Indus (Sind). In the West it is called Hinduism, though it is called *Sanatan Dharma* by Hindus. Now it is commonly known as 'Hindu Dharma'.

▲ Krishna is painted in blue to show that he is an avatar (incarnation) of God Vishnu. Dressed as a prince, he plays a love song on his flute, telling of his love for all creation and calling worshippers to love him.

No single person founded Hinduism. Over the centuries many religious thinkers developed the Hindu way of life. Hindus believe that all living beings are part of the Supreme Being, God, and will eventually be united with that Supreme Being. They believe that until they become one with the Supreme Being they have to live out countless lives, to be born, die and then be reborn again.

Gods and the Supreme Being

Many years ago, each village had its own village god and stories about that god. Travellers staying in a village would listen to these stories and then pass them on as they travelled. Soon, villagers adopted the gods (also called deities) of other villages.

Because there are so many Hindu gods, some people think that Hindus worship many gods. This is not the case. Hindus believe that all the gods are different aspects of the Supreme Being, a holy spirit who does not have any form. When they worship a god, they worship a particular aspect of the Supreme Being: for example god the loving mother, god the caring father, god the guiding teacher, god the friend, and so on.

Who is Krishna?

The name Krishna means 'the attractive one'. In Tamil Nadu, in South India, there are ancient stories and drawings of a black god who played his flute to cowherds. In North India, there are stories and drawings of a blue god called Krishna, who was an earthly prince and an incarnation of one of the most important Hindu gods, Vishnu. These legends have combined to make up the legend of Krishna, the cowherd prince.

Many followers of Krishna believe that he is not just one part of the Supreme Being, but that he is the Supreme Being: God. They live a life of worship and devotion to Krishna. Their aim is to become his devotees and to escape from the cycle of birth, death and rebirth.

Hindus believe that Krishna was born and lived in India. Places that are important to Hindus are shown below. ▼

WHO WAS THE LEADER?

Hindus believe that Krishna lived about 5,000 years ago. They also believe that he was an avatar (incarnation) of Vishnu sent to save the world from evil. Krishna started life as a cowherd. Later, he overthrew the evil King Kamsa. Eventually he moved his kingdom from Mathura, near Delhi, to Dwarka in Gujarat.

The question of whether Krishna was a real prince, or a character from mythology, has yet to be answered. The present-day city of Dwarka is not Krishna's city. The ruins of that city have never been found: they are believed to be under the sea.

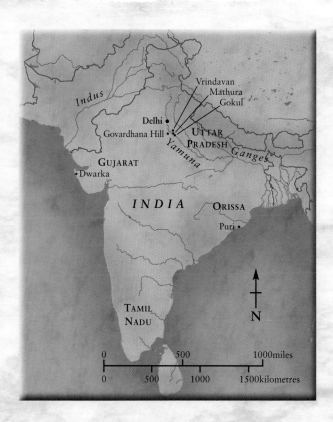

The Life of Krishna

The birth and childhood of Krishna

Thousands of years ago, an evil King called Kamsa ruled the kingdom of Mathura in north India. He was a cruel and evil ruler. He would summon demons and torture his subjects just for fun. Everybody lived in terror of him but nobody was powerful enough to overthrow him.

Kamsa believed he was immortal and would live forever. Then one day the king was told that he could only be killed by the eighth son of his cousin's sister, Devaki. Kamsa immediately threw Devaki and her husband, Vasudeva, into prison and killed every one of their children. When Krishna, their eighth son, was born, the gates of the prison magically opened. Vasudeva smuggled the baby out of the prison. He saw Yasoda, from a cowherds' village, sleeping by the banks of the Yamuna river. She had just given birth to a baby. Vasudeva swapped the two babies. When Yasoda woke she thought Krishna was her baby, and she and her husband, Nanda, brought Krishna up among the cowherds. Both Nanda and Yasoda did not know that Krishna was not their son, let alone that he was an avatar of God Vishnu.

Kamsa believed he had slain all the children of Devaki and Vasudeva. Then one day someone told him that Krishna was alive and would one

WHAT IS AN AVATAR?

Avatar is a Hindu word for a god who appears in the body of a person or an animal. Hindus believe that whenever there is evil on earth, the god Vishnu comes down to earth to save the world from evil. When he does this he assumes another form. He has come as a fish, a tortoise, a boar, a man-lion and in human form as Rama, Krishna and Buddha. Vishnu is said to have come to earth as an avatar nine times. It is said he will come again one final time.

▲ This traditional picture shows scenes from Krishna's early life. Top left, Krishna climbs on to the shoulders of the village children to steal butter which had been put out of his reach. Bottom right, his mother, Yasoda, scolds him. Bottom left, Krishna allows himself to be tied up by her as a punishment.

day kill him. Kamsa sent demons to the village to try and kill the baby Krishna. The demoness, Putana, came disguised as a beautiful woman to poison him. Despite being a baby, Krishna knew who she was and sucked her life from her.

Krishna was both a naughty child and a powerful god. Throughout his childhood he was always amusing and frustrating the villagers with his pranks. He would steal butter, his favourite food. He would untie the calves and watch everybody trying to catch them. Time and time again Yasoda would try to punish the naughty infant. She did not know that her son was more powerful than she was. Each time, Krishna would eventually submit to her punishment because he loved her.

Krishna the cowherd and lover

Krishna grew up a handsome young man. As he was Vishnu, the Supreme Being in human form, he inspired love from everybody. The cowherds and milkmaids he was brought up with did not know he was a god and they loved him as a son, a friend and as a boyfriend.

Krishna was good looking. He had long dark hair and soulful brown eyes. He played the flute. He was good fun. It was not surprising that all the young *gopis* (milkmaids) fell in love with him. Every morning the *gopis* would wake up and make a shrine to the goddess, 'Devi Katyayani', and bring her offerings of flowers, incense, fruit and rice. Then they would all offer up with the same prayer: 'Goddess Devi Katyayani, make Krishna, the blue cowherd, my husband.' All day they would sing love songs to him while they went about their business, milking the cows.

◄ An Indian painting of the handsome Krishna charming the *gopis*. Krishna is drawn in black in South India.

The most beautiful of the *gopis* was called Radha. Krishna fell in love with her. He would play the flute to her while she was milking the cows. Radha had a sense of humour and fun and this appealed to Krishna. He decided to play a trick on her.

He hid behind some bushes with a group of his friends. When Radha and her friends passed they jumped out and threw paint all over the women. Radha was quick to grab some paint and throw it all over Krishna. Soon everybody was covered in paint.

That night, Krishna played his flute and Radha came to him. Together they danced. She loved him so much she wanted to get married. But soon, events were to end Krishna's idyllic life among the cowherds.

▲ Nobody loved Krishna more than Radha. Her image stands beside Krishna in most of his temples and worshippers of Krishna will often ask Radha to help them seek Krishna's love and favour.

DANCES OF DEVOTION

Dance plays an important part in the worship of Krishna. Indian dance is done barefoot and there are strict rules about the correct facial expressions, hand movements and footwork. The most famous dance to Krishna is called the *Rasa* dance. This tells the story of Krishna dancing in the woods with the *gopis*. One of the styles of dance is the *Odissi*, which is performed in temples (called *mandirs* by Hindus). This dance tells the story of Krishna and Radha's love.

The cowherds' champion

One day Krishna went to the forest with the other cowherds, taking the cattle for grazing as usual. They became absorbed in a game but, after a while, realized that the cows and calves had strayed away. The cattle could not be seen anywhere and there was panic among the boys.

Krishna took pity on them. He called out the names of the cows. They had gone in search of fresh pasture, but while they were busy grazing a forest fire took hold. The cows cried out in distress. Hearing Krishna call out to them, the cows mooed back in reply, far away. There was agony in their cries. No one could hear them but Krishna. Krishna led the boys in the right direction. To their surprise, they found a heavy fire had surrounded the cattle. The boys pleaded with Krishna to help them.

Krishna said: 'Don't be afraid. Close your eyes, and don't open them until I ask you.' Krishna sucked all the fire towards himself and swallowed it entirely. Then he said: 'Now open your eyes, my friends.' The boys saw that they were back where they had been playing and all the cows were safe with them.

Krishna swallowed the flames before the cattle were harmed. The cowherds still did not realize that Krishna was not a cowherd but a god. ▼

This 1,000-year-old illustration shows Krishna killing King Kamsa. It comes from one of the Hindu scriptures that tells the life story of Krishna. ▶

Kamsa wanted to bring about Krishna's death, so he challenged Krishna to fight with a mighty wrestler, called Chanura. Krishna accepted the challenge and got into a chariot sent by Kamsa, with many of his cowherds. Watched by the cowherds in Kamsa's court, Krishna wrestled with Chanura. When Chanura took out a poisoned dagger to stab Krishna in the ankle, Krishna ducked and Chanura accidentally killed himself. Then Krishna grabbed Kamsa by the hair and swung him round and round. With a stamp of his foot, Krishna opened up the earth and flung Kamsa down into a fiery pit.

Everyone was overjoyed that Kamsa was dead. Krishna freed Devaki and Vasudeva from prison and they acknowledged him as their son.

RADHA

There are a number of stories, songs and dances about what happened to Radha. One song says that when her beloved became king she knew she could never marry him. So great was her love for Krishna she could love no other. She drowned herself in the river Ganges. However her love for Krishna was so great she could not die and the gods took her into the heavens and made her one of them. Today, in temples, she sits beside Krishna as his consort and worshippers approach her to win Krishna's love.

Krishna the prince

Amongst great rejoicing, Krishna brought the true king, Ugrasena, back to the throne of Mathura. Krishna was now to be a great warrior and prince. He could no longer live with the cowherds. He said a sad farewell to his friends from the village and his foster parents.

It was not long before the kingdom was under attack. Kamsa's queen sought revenge for her husband's death and persuaded her brother, Jarasandha, a powerful king, to march on Mathura. A fierce battle was fought and Krishna drove Jarasandha away. However, Jarasandha was bent on destroying Krishna and every year he returned with his army.

After eighteen years of war, Krishna decided that he no longer wanted to subject his people to a yearly battle. He decided to move the kingdom to the western coast of India and built a beautiful city, named Dwarka.

A beautiful princess, Rukmini, heard of Krishna's fame and fell in love with him. Her brother had arranged her marriage with another prince, without her consent. But Krishna came in a chariot driven by blue stallions and took Rukmini to be his queen. Soon other princesses all over India fell in love with the young prince.

◀ In a battle, Krishna throws the discus, a traditional weapon associated with the god Vishnu.

RUKMINI

Rukmini is said to be an avatar of the goddess Lakshmi, the consort of Vishnu. There is usually a temple dedicated to her next door to Krishna's temple, or her image stands close to that of Krishna.

Rukmini and Krishna on the way to their wedding. ▶

Krishna became a respected prince. When kings had disputes they would send for Krishna to help to sort them out. When the kings met they always looked to Krishna to lead the worship and discussions. Wise men travelled a long way to take advantage of Krishna's wisdom. Art, music and literature flourished in Dwarka under Krishna.

Krishna ruled Dwarka for 100 years. It seemed that he was immortal and his earthly life would never end. Then one day Krishna's people drank too much wine, and in a drunken brawl killed each other. Krishna alone survived and sat under a tree meditating. A hunter saw his foot, mistook him for a deer, and fired an arrow which pierced his heel. Thus, Krishna's earthly life had ended. As an avatar, he had helped to protect the good, destroy the evil, and re-establish the righteous life (Dharma).

Nothing of Krishna remained on earth. When he died his body became like a bright light and disappeared. He left no earthly descendants as his family were all dead. Soon after Krishna's death, the sea swallowed up his city of Dwarka. All that remains are the stories about his life.

The Sacred Texts

Krishna in the Hindu scriptures

Many religions have just one Holy book. In Hinduism there are a huge number of sacred texts that were written as early as 3000BCE, right through to modern times. These texts were written in a language called Sanskrit, which is the ancient language of India. It is considered to be the root of all languages and is still being used.

▲ The *Rig Veda* is one of the earliest Hindu scriptures. This was written in the area around the Indus Valley by the earliest Hindu believers. The Sanskrit language it is written in is as old as the scriptures and is still used in India today.

These Hindu texts are a mixture of thought and legend about the various Hindu gods and religious practices that worshippers should carry out in their everyday lives and worship. These texts were based on teachings that were handed on from generation to generation until they were written down.

First stories of Krishna

Stories about Krishna and Krishna's religious philosophy do not appear in the early Hindu scriptures. The earliest mention of Krishna is in the great Indian epic poem, the *Mahabharata*, which was written around the period of 3000BCE. In this poem Krishna is the respected prince of Dwarka. There is no reference to his earlier life as a cowherd.

The stories of Krishna, the cowherd, and his mission to slay King Kamsa are part of a collection of stories

AUM

This ancient Hindu symbol and sound is called *AUM*. You can see it in Hindu temples, drawings and even on Western fashions and jewellery.

This symbol is said to be the meaning of life, the Supreme Being. All prayers to Krishna begin and end with *AUM*. It is considered to be a holy sound.

'Aum the eternal word is all: what was, what is, what shall be, and what is beyond eternity. All is Aum.'

Upanishad

about the gods called the *Bhagavatam*. Other ancient stories about Krishna, called the *Puranas*, were written down later. Devout Hindus consider these stories to be their spiritual history and not myths. There are eighteen big and eighteen small *Puranas*.

Krishna is unique among the Hindu gods in that he inspired a whole culture of sacred literature and songs with a popular appeal. In fact, a whole ancient 'pop' culture was inspired by Krishna. Famous songs, poems and dances tell stories from his life and his teachings. Hinduism regards any writing, dance or song that inspires devotion as sacred. These are often performed in temples. It is these songs, poems and pictures that tell us of Krishna's love for Radha.

▲ A Hindu priest, sitting in front of the symbol for *AUM*. The food on the tray beside him is *prashad*, food which has been offered to the god (see pages 30–31).

The Mahabharata

The *Mahabharata* is the longest poem in the world with
100,000 verses. *Bharat* is the old name for India and
Mahabharata means 'the history of Great India'.

An epic feud

This epic poem tells the story of the feud between two
groups of people: the Pandavas and the Kauravas. The
feud began when King Dhritarastra, who was born blind,
handed his throne to his brother, Pandu. The Pandavas
were the sons of Pandu, and the Kauravas were the sons of
Dhritarastra. Their feud was over who should rule the
country after the death of Pandu. Krishna, the prince of
Dwarka, was a cousin of the Pandavas and the Kauravas
and was often asked to negotiate between the two parties.

The feud took place over decades and various
solutions were tried to resolve the problem.
Initially, the Pandavas were given one part of
the kingdom and the Kauravas another. When
the Pandava kingdom became more
prosperous, the Kauravas wanted it back.
A game of dice was arranged to
decide who would get all of the
kingdom. The Kauravas cheated
and won the game. As a result, the
Pandavas were sent into exile
for thirteen years.

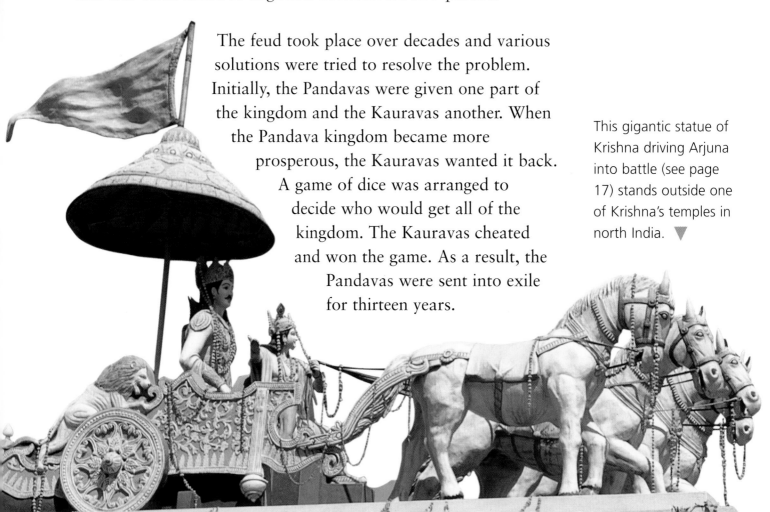

This gigantic statue of
Krishna driving Arjuna
into battle (see page
17) stands outside one
of Krishna's temples in
north India. ▼

THE MAHABHARATA IN POPULAR CULTURE

Throughout the ages many Hindus could not read but this did not prevent them having access to the *Mahabharata*. Companies of actors and dancers would travel across India and perform stories from the epic. Performances would start at about 7pm and go on through the night to 7am!

In modern India, the *Mahabharata* inspires films and television dramas. The Indian film industry has made countless versions of the epic, lasting for many hours. Audiences gather in huge outdoor cinemas and watch the film through the night.

▲ Shooting a scene from the *Mahabharata* for an Indian television programme.

The battle of Kurukshetra

After thirteen years the Pandavas returned from exile and demanded their kingdom. It was clear by then that only a battle would decide the outcome. Before this great battle at Kurukshetra, both sides asked Krishna to fight with them. Krishna gave them the choice of having him (but he would not fight) or having his army, which would fight. The Pandavas chose him and the Kauravas chose his army.

One of King Pandu's sons was called Arjuna. He was also Krishna's cousin. During the battle, Krishna drove a chariot for Arjuna, and advised him on the battlefield.

Krishna's advice won the battle for the Pandavas and the eldest, Prince Yudhisthira, was crowned emperor of India.

The Bhagavad Gita

In the main story of the *Mahabharata*, ancient legends are retold but there are also long sections of explanation. The *Bhagavad Gita* is eighteen chapters of the *Mahabharata* and, to many readers, it is the most important part. Some scholars believe that the *Gita* was added at a later date to include the teachings of Krishna.

Krishna's teachings

Bhagavad means 'the sermon of the Blessed One', and the *Gita* is the song of Krishna.

The *Bhagavad Gita* is the only place that we find Krishna's teachings. They are respected and followed as the words of God, delivered by a god of love who is showing all Hindus a way to become one with him, the Supreme Being, through loving him.

▲ Driving a chariot was the most dangerous job on a battlefield. In the middle of the battle, Krishna gave the teachings of the *Gita* to Arjuna.

The *Bhagavad Gita* is a series of conversations between Arjuna and Krishna (who was acting as Arjuna's charioteer) during the battle of Kurukshetra. They are about the meaning of life and the way to salvation. During this conversation on the battlefield, Krishna reveals himself as God, the Supreme Being.

The holy book of India

Many Hindus believe that the *Gita* is the most important words of God. Hindu leaders and thinkers throughout

history, and to the present day, have used the *Gita* as an inspiration for their thoughts and actions.

Although there are many holy scriptures, the *Bhagavad Gita* is considered the holy book of India. In India, it is used when taking an oath of office and in the law courts, in the same way the Bible is used in Western countries.

▲ An Indian holy man will read the *Gita* countless times to try and know more about Krishna.

Mahatma Gandhi wore simple clothes, to show his equality with people from all classes. ▼

MAHATMA GANDHI

The teachings in the *Gita* influenced modern India. Mahatma Gandhi, who led India towards independence from the British in 1947, read the *Gita* every day. He believed that every one of his actions was for God.

Krishna's Teachings

Krishna is the Supreme Being

The most important message of the *Bhagavad Gita* is that Krishna is the Supreme Being, not just one aspect of that Being. Krishna reveals himself to Arjuna as the Supreme Being and Arjuna recognizes him as such. So, Krishna's teaching in the *Gita* is therefore the word of God, delivered by God.

God in human form

Krishna lived in human form. This is seen as proof that the Supreme Being is present in people, and in every aspect of human life. He is there in Krishna the warrior and the prince, but he is also there in the cowherd, one of the lowly people in society. The Supreme Being is there in the actions of a naughty child who is punished, a handsome young man and lover, a wise prince, a mighty warrior and a philosopher. This is proof that the Supreme Being is in all people and all people can become one with that Being, Krishna.

▲ Even as a naughty child, Krishna was believed to be the Supreme Being.

Everyone is reborn

The *Gita* begins with Arjuna on the battlefield, facing his cousins in battle, knowing that he will have to kill them. He is reluctant to do that. This prompts Krishna to explain to Arjuna that he cannot kill what is eternal. Because every spirit is part of the Supreme Being they are eternal and can never die.

Hindus are cremated when they die and their ashes are immersed in a sacred river. ▼

So if Arjuna kills someone in battle, that person would not really die. They would either be reborn in another body, or become one with the Supreme Being.

REINCARNATION

'As a man throws away used and worn out clothes after death to enter new ones, so does the spirit leave worn out bodies after death to enter new ones'

Bhagavad Gita, 2(22)

The idea that a spirit or soul is reborn in another body after death is an old Hindu belief called reincarnation. Hindus believe that they are reborn as another human being or even as another creature. The outcome depends on the actions of a person in his or her life. It is every Hindu's aim eventually to escape from being reborn on earth and to be united with the Supreme Being.

How to become one with Krishna

The main question in Hinduism is how to unite with the Supreme Being and escape from being reborn again and again. In the *Gita*, Krishna tells Arjuna of the different ways that people can unite or become one with the Supreme Being.

Yoga

Hindus have a special word for unite. That word is 'yoga'. In the West, we think of yoga as doing exercises to free our minds from stress and to relax our bodies. In Hindu thought, yoga means a lot more than just doing exercises. Yoga exercise is only one of many ways that you can clear

▲ A Hindu holy man, or *sadhu*, in India. *Sadhus* spend their entire lives practising the various forms of yoga, seeking to unite with the Supreme Being.

your mind of distractions and unite with God. Many Hindus are totally devoted to practising the different forms of yoga in a quest to unite with the Supreme Being. Priests read the scriptures, practise yoga exercises, chant mantras and pray.

Yoga for all

In the *Gita*, Krishna gives ordinary people ways they can unite with him, the Supreme Being, and still live their everyday lives. The key is to live doing every action for Krishna. This is called *karma-yoga*. They also have to live lives of devotion or *bhakti-yoga*.

The way Krishna related to ordinary, lowly people was a big step forward in Hindu thought. His teaching meant that salvation was now possible for everybody, not just priests or holy men.

A *sannyasin* meditating at a Hindu temple. ▼

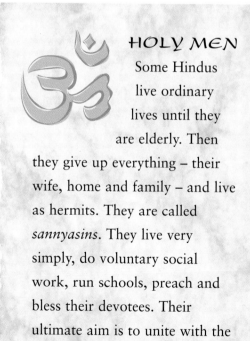

HOLY MEN

Some Hindus live ordinary lives until they are elderly. Then they give up everything – their wife, home and family – and live as hermits. They are called *sannyasins*. They live very simply, do voluntary social work, run schools, preach and bless their devotees. Their ultimate aim is to unite with the Supreme Being.

Karma-yoga: every action must be done for Krishna

Karma is the Hindu law of cause and effect. It is the belief that if you do a good deed you will make good *karma* and good things will follow. If you do a bad action, you will make bad *karma* and bad things will happen. Hindus believe that no one can escape this. Hindus, therefore, try to avoid doing bad things to avoid being reborn in poverty or as another life form.

▲ Many people in India live in terrible poverty. Hindus believe that by trying to live a life of devotion to Krishna, they will avoid poverty in a later life.

Arjuna and *karma*

In the *Gita*, Arjuna worries that if he kills people, he will bring about bad *karma*. Krishna tells him that he is not responsible for killing others because he belongs to the class of people called the warriors. It is therefore his duty to fight in battle in order to remove evil and establish Dharma (good rule). To do his duty will not create bad *karma*.

Doing everything out of love for Krishna

Krishna has a strong message about *karma*. Whatever we do, we create *karma*, good or bad. If we worry about every action, that worry ties us to the world. To attain release from the cycle of birth, disease, old age, death and rebirth people must stop worrying about whether they have done a good or a bad thing.

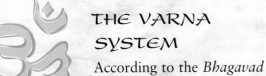

THE VARNA SYSTEM

According to the *Bhagavad Gita*, there are four varnas, or groups, of people. They were created by God, and are based on a person's inborn qualities, and the work associated with them. The four varnas are:

Brahmin: intellectuals (teachers, priests, guides/advisors, etc.)

Kshatriya: warriors (soldiers, police, administrators, etc.)

Vaishya: business people, traders, farmers, etc.

Shudra: manual workers.

The varna system is based on Hinduism and it is nothing to do with the so-called caste system. Caste is a word that was used by invaders to divide Hindu society, including Muslims and Christians. The British government in India created a class of people called 'untouchables' in order to divide and rule the people. These people were limited by very strict rules as to what they could do, who they could have contact with, and where they could go. However, in 1947, after India gained independence, the new government abolished untouchability. It is now considered offensive to use this word.

By devotion to Krishna there is another, better option. If a person does all their actions out of love of Krishna they have risen above concerns over good and bad *karma*. Their actions will bring them closer to the Supreme Being.

By doing everything out of love for Krishna, his followers believe that they will come closer to the Supreme Being. ▼

A life of devotion to Krishna: bhakti-yoga

According to Krishna, *bhakti-yoga* is the greatest form of yoga and the best way to unite with Him, the Supreme Being. *Bhakti-yoga* means devotion. To practise *bhakti-yoga*, Krishna must be at the centre of a person's life. Every action – eating, praying, dancing, painting or working – must be an act of devotion to Krishna.

A god of love

Krishna's teaching about *bhakti yoga* is radical because it accepts all people, however grand or lowly. In the *Gita*, Krishna says he will accept anything that is given to him in

Making music can be an act of devotion to Krishna. These traditional instruments are being played in a Krishna temple in North India. ▼

A shrine to Krishna in a family's living room, in the UK. It is decorated with pictures of Krishna and lit with lights to celebrate the Hindu festival of Diwali (see page 42). ▶

love, whoever offers it. It could be offered by a priest, a king or the lowliest of people. (Once a devotee was so overcome by his love he accidentally offered Krishna banana skins instead of the bananas. Krishna is said to have eaten the skins with relish as they were offered in love.)

The influence of Krishna on Hindu thought is as a God of Love who loves the humble people such as village peasants, and accepts their offerings as equal to other offerings.

It is easy to see how Krishna's teaching on *bhakti-yoga* has influenced his worshippers. Every devotee has a shrine to Krishna in his or her home, and Krishna is at the centre of all family life. People carry out their daily tasks out of love for Krishna. The god has also inspired beautiful art, dance and music. Religious thinkers have spent years writing books about Krishna. Political leaders who followed Mahatma Gandhi (see page 19), have been influenced by the teachings in the *Gita* and have used them to fight for a better world for all.

EQUALITY IN DEVOTION

'Whatever a person may offer,
Be it a leaf, a flower, fruit or even water,
That I willingly accept
For it was given in love.'

Bhagavad Gita 5(26)

Krishna would accept an offering from anybody, whatever their social standing and however humble the offering, as long as it was offered in love.

Krishna and Food

Krishna, the lord of the cows

Krishna was brought up as a cowherd and cows were very dear to him. One of the names given to Krishna is *Gopala*, which means 'Lord of the Cows'.

Cows are sacred

To Krishna and other Hindus, the cow is sacred because she is the symbol of Mother Earth. The cow provides humankind with milk and other dairy foods to help them stay healthy. The bull helps plough the land and do other heavy work. He is considered the symbol of Dharma in that he gives more than he takes.

Pictures of Krishna often show him with cows that are richly adorned with garlands round their necks and peacock feathers on their heads. These modern cows have been covered in gold decorations for a festival. ▼

COWS

"All who eat the flesh or permit the slaughter of cows will rot in hell for as many years as there are hairs on the cow's body."

Puranas

Hindus believe that to kill and eat the flesh of a cow or her calf is the most terrible sin they can commit. Until recent times, Hindus were totally dependent on farming and cattle breeding, so killing a cow would threaten people's needs.

▲ Indian people who do not have cars, trucks or farm machinery still rely on bulls in many aspects of their daily lives.

In the *Bhagavad Gita*, Krishna states that cows are helpless and need to be protected. Many pictures of Krishna show him caring for cows who in turn look lovingly at him.

Hindus believe that in return for love and care, cows will reward people with milk and other dairy products: butter, yoghurt and ghee. These are regarded as the most nourishing foods. Cow dung and urine are also used to purify as they have antiseptic qualities.

Hindus therefore forbid the eating of beef. Most Hindus respect all life and are vegetarians. Even those Hindus who do eat some meat will never eat beef, so Hindu butchers do not sell it. In India, cows are allowed to roam free and live out their natural life. A garlanded cow, peacefully lying down in a busy city causing a traffic jam, used to be a common sight in India. Now it is rare in modern cities, where cows are kept away from busy streets in sanctuaries.

Food for Krishna

Devotees of Krishna always try to prepare Krishna's favourite food to offer him. The tales of Krishna's childhood tell of his love for dairy products. As a child, the young Krishna would do anything to eat his favourite food. He was called 'the butter thief' by the villagers.

As a child, Krishna would steal pots of butter to eat. No place was safe to hide it from him. ▼

In the *Bhagavad Gita*, Krishna talks about vegetarianism. He sees all life forms as being part of the Supreme Being and worthy of equal love and respect. The Gita lists healthy foods other than meat: dairy products, grains, fruits and vegetables.

Food that is prepared for Krishna is made with love in spotless conditions. Surfaces are carefully wiped before food preparation starts. Only the best ingredients are used. A person preparing the food won't even taste it before offering it to Krishna in case it becomes spoiled.

Prashad

Food that is prepared and offered to Krishna is called *prashad* and is sacred food. *Prashad* means 'the mercy of God'. Devotees believe that Krishna blesses the food and that *prashad* food is full of

PRASHAD
*If you eat ordinary food
you develop lusty desires
to enjoy the material
world; if you eat prashad
you increase your love of
God with every mouthful.*

A belief amongst devotees
of Krishna

◀ Food forms an
important part of Hindu
worship. A variety of food
is always offered to
Krishna, especially at
festivals.

Krishna's mercy. At home, food is initially offered to
Krishna, either at the shrine when it becomes *prashad*, or
when it is shared out amongst the family. In temples, food
is first offered to the deity and then shared out among
worshippers. Devotees of Krishna will only eat food which
is *prashad*.

The Sacred Places

Pilgrimages

There are a number of sacred places in India that Hindus visit on pilgrimages. Many of these are rivers such as the Ganges. Hindus also go to places associated with events in a god's life, or famous temples connected to that deity.

Women pilgrims, on their way to the festival of *Maha-Kumba*. ▼

Reasons for pilgrimages

Hindus go on pilgrimages for many different reasons. They frequently go to a sacred river to bathe in the waters and purify themselves. If a loved one has died they go to scatter or immerse their ashes in the river. Another reason for a pilgrimage is to make amends for a wrongdoing. Some people take a vow to go on a pilgrimage if something they want very much happens, such as the birth of a child.

SACRED RIVERS

The Ganges is the most sacred river in India. A story says it was created by the god Vishnu. He pierced the earth with his toenail and the pure waters gushed out. Ganges water is said to have purifying powers. Hindus aim to die by the Ganges as they believe they will be set free if they do.

There are seven holy rivers in India, and the Yamuna is one associated with Krishna and Radha. The place where both the rivers merge is where the festival of *Maha-Kumba* takes place once every twelve years.

Hindus also go on a pilgrimage to be healed from an illness or disability. It is believed Hindu shrines associated with holy men have healing powers. This is because Hindus believe that God will forgive past sins if people truly try to make amends, under the guidance of a holy man. The best way to cope is to live a good life. This helps to avoid a repeat of the illness or disability in another life.

People who are particularly devoted to Krishna go on a pilgrimage to places associated with him. They might visit places where they believe he lived during his earthly life. Or they might visit a famous temple during a festival. There are temples dedicated to Krishna all over India, and in other countries, such as Britain, Canada and the USA. Pilgrimages such as these are ways of focusing on Krishna, and are seen as acts of devotion.

▲ The Yamuna river, at Vrindavan (see page 34). Hindus on a pilgrimage bathe in sacred rivers.

Sacred places

The most important holy places connected to Krishna are his birth place, Mathura; Gokul, where he was brought up as a cowherd; Vrindavan, where he played with the *gopis*; and Dwarka (even though it is not Krishna's actual city). Another sacred place is Puri, which has a famous Krishna temple and a yearly festival which honours Krishna as Jagannath, the Lord of the Universe. In many of his temples, Krishna has a local name. In Dwarka, he is called Lord Dwarkadeesh. In Puri, Krishna is Lord Jagannath.

Vrindavan

The most beautiful place associated with Krishna is Vrindavan, which is close to Mathura. It is a rural area and there is a sense of peace and beauty about it. There are many temples to Krishna and Radha in the area, and a number of festivals that draw pilgrims to visit the temples. These festivals remember events that happened to Krishna during his life as a cowherd.

The Govind Dev temple at Vrindavan, rising above the trees. Hindu temples are built high so that pilgrims can see them from a distance and find them easily. ▼

Govardhana Hill

Near Vrindavan is Govardhana Hill which is sacred to Krishna. It is said that he lifted this hill to shelter villagers from torrential rain sent by the god Indra. (See page 42.)

Dwarka

The present-day city of Dwarka is on the western tip of Gujarat. It is a small city and nothing like the city Krishna ruled. The main temple of Krishna is one of the most important temples dedicated to Krishna. The temple has an image of Krishna called Dwarkadeesh. To worshippers, Lord Dwarkadeesh displays all of Krishna's achievements in the arts, politics and philosophy.

Outside the city is a second temple to Rukmini, Krishna's queen. There she is worshipped not only as Krishna's wife but also as an avatar of Vishnu's wife, Lakshmi.

VISITING THE TEMPLE AT DWARKA

Non-Hindus are restricted from entering many Krishna temples. Before they are allowed to enter the temple at Dwarka, non-Hindus have to fill in a form to prove that they have some commitment to Hinduism and Krishna. Once the form is filled in they must prove their devotion to Krishna by presenting Lord Dwarkadeesh with an offering or a prayer.

▲ Even though present-day Dwarka is in a different place from Krishna's city, it is home to a large temple where followers of Krishna come to worship and celebrate festivals.

Festivals

A calendar of festivals

One way Hindus practise *bhakti-yoga* (see page 26) is to remember the avatars' birthdays, special days, and stories about their lives. It is therefore not surprising that the Hindu calendar is full of festivals. There is hardly a day when there isn't a festival celebrating the achievements of one of the Hindu deities.

Celebrations vary from area to area. Even the best known Hindu festivals such as *Deepawali* (Diwali) and Holi are celebrated in different ways, and different stories are remembered depending on which deity the town or village favours. Devotees of Krishna will celebrate Krishna's life at all the Hindu festivals as well as celebrating his birthday, marriage and victory over evil.

The *Maha-Kumba* festival in Uttar Pradesh takes place only every twelve years, but it attracts millions of people. ▼

PREPARING THE TEMPLE DEITIES

During festivals and worship the image of the god in the temple is always given a purifying bath in milk and holy water from a sacred river. After this, the image is dressed in new festive clothes.

Preparing for a festival can take days. At home, the family will prepare a feast for the god, consisting of his or her favourite food and lots of sweets. Preparations by priests in the temple will mirror the preparations at home, but on a wider scale. The priests and many devotees will also prepare for the festival by fasting and reading the sacred texts.

Festivals can go on for a period of days. During this time there is worship in the temple. Dancers and actors will give performances of the stories being remembered by the festival.

Festivals and special days are some of the few times that the images of the deities leave the temples. During festivals the temple deities are sometimes taken out on carts and driven round the town. During some festivals, giant images of the deity are made and paraded round the town. At the end of the festivities they are submerged in a holy river or lake.

▲ Temple gods are beautifully dressed for a festival. Dressing and washing the images is a sacred task and only the head priest and a few assistants are allowed to touch them, change their clothes and brush their hair. This young priest is lighting a lamp for the festival of Diwali (see page 42).

Throwing colourful paint is a feature of Holi. There may also be fireworks and bonfires.

Festivals of Krishna

Holi (February/March)
Holi is celebrated on the day of the full moon in the Hindu month of Phalguna. It is a spring festival and is celebrated all over India. It is a time to wear your oldest clothes as people throw coloured powder or coloured water over each other at Holi. The mischievous Krishna is behind the tradition of colour throwing. (See page 9.)

Jagannath Festival (June/July)
This festival is held at the temple in Puri which is in Orissa, east India. It occurs on the first day of the new moon in the month of Asadha. Pilgrims from all over India travel to Puri for this festival.

THE HINDU CALENDAR
The Hindu calendar is different from other calendars. It does have twelve months but each month is split in two halves, the bright half and the dark half, according to the cycle of the moon. As the appearance of the moon decides when months begin and end the festivals occur on different dates each year.

The festival celebrates Krishna as Lord Jagannath, the Lord of the Universe. It remembers his march from the city of Dwarka to Kurukshetra as a pilgrimage. To the sound of loud gongs, giant images of Krishna and his brother and sister are placed on enormous decorated wooden chariots with colourful canopies. The Raja (prince) of Puri does the job of a sanitary worker and sweeps the ground in front of the chariots to show that all people are equal in Krishna's eyes.

It takes about 4,000 people to pull each of the three chariots to the other end of the town where they spend a week. Each day, the images are dressed in new clothes and freshly cooked food is offered and shared as *prashad*. At the end of the week they are taken back to the temple.

The three giant chariots at Puri are about 13 metres high and have eighteen wheels. ▼

FOOD FOR PILGRIMS

Pilgrims often walk great distances to the festival at Puri, as receiving the food that has been offered to Krishna during the festival is of great importance to them. The priests at the temple cook chick-pea and dried-fruit balls the size of Lord Jagannath's fist, which are shared out. These are often eaten on the long journey home.

The Swing Festival (July/August)

Vrindavan is the place to be for this lovely festival that celebrates Krishna and Radha's love. This is one of the longer festivals, lasting for thirteen days. In all the temples, the images of Krishna and Radha are put on to gold and silver swings. In Orissa, there are wonderful temple dances that tell of the great love between Krishna and Radha.

Janmashtami (August/September)

This festival celebrates Krishna's birth and takes place all over India. In the days leading up to the festival, most devotees pray and fast to prepare. Fasting helps to focus one's mind on Krishna without the distractions of food. The fast also helps people to remember that there was evil in the world before Krishna was born, and that Krishna came to save the world from evil. The fast ends on a new-moon night at midnight, the hour of Krishna's birth.

All over India, worshippers flock to Krishna temples to worship together at midnight. In many temples, the image of the deity will be washed in holy water from a sacred river, then purified with milk and honey. The deity is then dressed in special clothes and placed in a cradle.

▲ Krishna and Radha on a swing in a temple at Vrindavan. The Swing Festival celebrates the beauty and love of Krishna and the great love that Radha had for him which all worshippers would like to share.

Pilgrims who travel to Mathura for this festival pay a special visit to Gokul, nearby. This is where Krishna's foster parents, Nanda and Yasoda, celebrated his birth 5,000 years ago. Pilgrims can see the house where they believe Krishna was raised, and the very cradle that the baby Krishna was placed in.

Radhastami (August/September)

This festival celebrates the birth of Radha and falls fifteen days after the birth of Krishna. Devotees will fast and then visit the temple with offerings for Radha. Every step is taken to please her, as devotees believe that she will put in a good word for them with Krishna.

CELEBRATING KRISHNA'S BIRTHDAY

Some Hindus believe that if they don't celebrate Krishna's birthday they will be reborn as a snake.

'If one neglects to celebrate the birthday of Lord Krishna, the Krishna Janmashtami, one will be reborn as a serpent in a deep forest.'

Bhavishya Purana

▲ *Janmashtami* worshippers make human pyramids to copy Krishna's daring when he stole the butter as a child.

Diwali (October/November)

Diwali is the most popular Hindu festival. It is celebrated during late autumn, when the evenings are getting darker. Lights are placed at every window and door. There are lots of different stories behind the Diwali celebrations that honour the different deities. There are different stories in various regions of India. Devotees of Krishna believe it was the time when Krishna killed Narakasura, the son of Bhumi, deity of the earth. Narakasura was a cruel demon who conquered all the planets, including the earth. When Narakasura was killed by Krishna, the demon's mother asked Krishna to make the day of her son's death a celebration of the triumph of good over evil.

Govardhana Hill Puja (October/November)

This festival remembers the time when Krishna ordered the cowherds not to give offerings to Indra, the king of the celestial angels who control rain, but to Govardhana Hill instead. Indra had become too proud. He was outraged and sent torrential rain which threatened to flood the villages. Krishna used this opportunity to prove that he

▲ Shops are decorated with lights as people shop for Diwali gifts of cards, sweets and other presents.

Krishna effortlessly lifts the hill like an umbrella to shelter the villagers and cattle from Indra's rain, proving he was a stronger god than Indra. ▶

was more powerful than Indra by lifting Govardhana Hill and holding it over the villages to shelter them.

During the festival devotees make hills out of cow dung or sacred food. They circle the hill in worship and then the food is shared. At Govardhana Hill, food is placed on the actual hill itself during the festival. This shows caring for the mountain and the environment. Mountains play an important part in keeping the balance in nature.

Gita Jayanti (December)

Hindus regard the *Bhagavad Gita* as the most sacred of their scriptures. The day that Krishna is said to have given the sermon of the *Gita* to Arjuna (on the battlefield at Kurukshetra) is celebrated every year as the birthday of the *Gita*. In Kurukshetra there is a yearly festival to mark this day.

COW DUNG

Hindus use cow dung to clean their homes and to purify temples before and during acts of worship. Cow dung might smell but it is proven to have antiseptic qualities and a medicinal value. It can be processed to make soap to cure skin diseases.

A woman carries cow dung home to use as fuel. ▶

Hinduism Today

Krishna in modern India

Wherever you go in India you cannot escape Krishna. He appeals to everybody from kings to the humble peasants. He is the God of love who loves everybody and attracts love in return.

▲ A street seller sells a variety of Hindu posters, books and cards. Krishna as a child, with a pot of butter, can be seen in the centre.

In the markets, stallholders sell cards and pictures of Krishna. The story of the *Mahabharata* is still a best seller in bookshops. It can also be bought as audio tapes and videos. Crowds still fill huge outdoor cinemas and sit into the night watching films based on the *Mahabharata*.

Krishna and politics

In the twentieth century, Krishna's teachings about equality became part of Indian politics.

Mahatma Gandhi, who was influenced by the *Bhagavad Gita*, called the lowly people *Harijan*, 'the children of God', and campaigned for an India where there was equality. The dreadful rules that divided people were abolished. By 1950 it was illegal for anybody to be treated as an 'untouchable'. Such people were able to enter temples, be educated and do jobs other than the unskilled tasks they traditionally did.

Krishna in the Western world

Hinduism is the third largest religion in the world with about 850,000,000 members. Of these, 95 per cent live in India. The reason why Hinduism has not spread throughout the world is because Hindus do not seek converts. When Hindus moved to places such as the USA, the Caribbean, Kenya, Britain and Canada, they always kept their faith and culture, but they did not try to change other people's faiths.

Krishna Consciousness

However, Hinduism was to attract Western devotees. In the 1960s, known as the hippie era, people in Britain and the USA were looking for a culture of peace and love. A Hindu guru and devotee of Krishna, Srila Bhaktivedanta Prabhupada, felt his mission was to bring Krishna Consciousness to the West. He arrived in the USA and started chanting in Tompkins Square Park. Many young people were attracted to his teachings on Krishna, and Krishna Consciousness, or ISKCON, was formed. Today there are ISKCON centres all over the world and devotees chanting 'Hare Krishna' in the streets are a familiar sight.

A god of love – for everyone

Why did Krishna penetrate Western culture? It could be argued that the idea of Krishna is not new to Western thought. Like Krishna, Jesus was God come down to live as a human being. Jesus also taught that everyone can be saved by loving a god of love.

Krishna brings a message of equality: that everyone is a part of the Supreme Being; everyone is eternal and can find salvation.

▲ George Harrison (left), Paul McCartney (centre) and Jane Asher (right) meet a Hindu guru, the Maharishi, in 1968.

KRISHNA IN THE TOP TEN

Many famous people were attracted to the teachings of Krishna. Beatle George Harrison was one. He wrote a song of devotion to Krishna called *My Sweet Lord*, which reached the top ten in the pop charts. He also donated a stately home to ISKCON: Bhaktivedanta Manor, north of London in the UK.

Glossary

Antiseptic Something that prevents the growth of organisms that cause disease.

Avatar A Hindu word that means 'to come down'. The god Vishnu comes down to earth as different forms, or avatars, to protect good and destroy evil.

BCE Before Christian Era. (A non-Christian version of BC.)

Bhagavad Gita The eighteen chapters of the *Mahabharata* that contain the teachings of Krishna.

Bhakti-yoga Living a life of devotion to God.

Consort A companion, wife or husband.

Cowherd Someone who looks after cows.

Cremated When a dead person's body is burned to ashes.

Demon A cruel, evil person: someone who is against God.

Dharma A religion or religious duty.

Discus A heavy, thick-centred disc, thrown as a weapon, or by an athlete.

Eternal Lasting for ever.

Foster parents Parents who bring up a child who is not their own by birth.

Ghee A type of butter, used in Indian cooking.

Gopis Milkmaids.

Holy Belonging to God, sacred.

Immortal Living for ever.

Incarnation A living form of a god or a spirit. (See Avatar.)

ISKCON International Society for Krishna Consciousness.

Karma-yoga Making sure everything you do is done for God.

Kauravas Krishna's cousins, the main characters of the *Mahabharata*; sons of King Dhritarastra.

Krishna An avatar of the Hindu god Vishnu. Many Hindus believe Krishna is the Supreme Being.

Kurukshetra The place where the great battle was fought between the Kauravas and the Pandavas in the *Mahabharata*.

Mahabharata The greatest Indian epic, and the longest poem in the world.

Mantras Verses or sounds that are repeated.

Pandavas Krishna's cousins, the main characters of the *Mahabharata*; sons of King Pandu.

Philosophy The study of what people think they know, of what they believe is real and of life.

Prashad Food that has been offered to Krishna.

Puranas Stories and teachings about different Hindu avatars.

Radha One of the *gopis* and Krishna's first love.

Reincarnation The belief that you die and are reborn in another life.

Sacred Connected to God; holy.

Salvation Escape from sin and its results.

Scriptures Sacred writings of a religion.

Shrine A holy place, sometimes containing a religious statue.

Sin A bad act.

Supreme Being How the Hindus describe God.

Vishnu The protector of the world and often considered a form of God.

Warrior A brave or experienced soldier or fighter.

Yoga The Hindu word which means 'to unite'. Relaxation exercises are called *Yoga Asana*.

Further Information

Books to read

Celebrate Hindu Festivals by Dilip Kadodwala and Paul Gateshill (Heinemann, 1995)
Hinduism by Dilip Kadodwala (Wayland, 1995)
Hindu Temple by Anita Ganeri (A and C Black, 1997)
Hindu Scriptures by V P Hemant Kanitkar (Heinemann, 1994)
Holi by Dilip Kadodwala (Evans, 1997)

Websites

http://www.iskcon.org
A comprehensive web page that contains prayers and meditations on Krishna, a summary of the *Gita*, cookery pages, pages on music, dance and art as well as information about ISKCON.

The Hindu Universe
http://www.hindunet.org
This web page features a Hindu calendar, a glossary of terms and information on Hindu arts, customs, worship and scripture. Links to other Hindu resources are also included.

Other media resources

BBC Education produces schools media resources on different faiths.
BBC Information
PO Box 1116, Belfast BT2 7AJ
Tel: 08700 100 222   email: info@bbc.co.uk
http://www.bbc.co.uk/schools

Channel 4 produces schools media resources on different faiths, including *Animated World Faiths*.
C4 Schools
PO Box 100, Warwick CV34 6TZ
Tel: 01926 436444
email:sales@schools.channel4.co.uk
http://www.channel4.com/schools

For further information, books and resources

The Institute of Indian Art and Culture
The Bhavan Centre, 4a Castletown Road
West Kensington, London W14 9HQ
Tel: 0207 381 3045

The Hindu Cultural Society
321 Colney Hatch Lane, London N11
Tel: 0208 361 4484

The Commonwealth Institute Resource Centre
Kensington High Street, London W8 6NQ
Tel: 0207 603 4535
http://www.commonwealth.org.uk

Hindu Sahitya Kendra (Hindu Literature Shop)
46–48 Loughborough Road, Leicester LE4 5LD
Tel: 0116 266 5665/261 1303
Fax: 0116 261 1931